49.95

TALISMANS

TALISMANS

Maudelle Driskell

The Hobblebush Granite State Poetry Series, Volume VIII

HOBBLEBUSH BOOKS

Brookline, New Hampshire

Composed in Adobe Arno Pro at Hobblebush Books

Printed in the United States of America

Cover illustration: "#6, from the Garden of the Phoenix series"; monotype; 2011; by Marie Pavlicek-Wehrli; www.mariepavlicek.com
Back cover author photo by E. Stokesbury

ISBN: 978-1-939449-03-0
Library of Congress Control Number: 2014934160

The Hobblebush Granite State Poetry Series, Volume VIII
Editors: Sidney Hall Jr. and Rodger Martin

HOBBLEBUSH BOOKS
17-A Old Milford Road
Brookline, New Hampshire 03033
www.hobblebush.com

*For my family—the biological,
the creative, and the chosen*

Contents

III

I

TALISMANS

At the flea market across from the Commerce speedway
you can buy Elvis relics in ziplock bags
with masking tape labels—the napkin smeared with peanut butter
and banana grease, the pocket comb with a single strand
of black hair twined in its teeth, rhinestones
dandruffed from the white Las Vegas jumpsuit. All point
with the insignificance of dogs that have already treed the coon
toward the masterpiece of the collection—Elvis's wart.

Showcased under the glass of an overturned jelly jar,
impaled on a bright-yellow balled stickpin stuck in a cork,
the wart, looking for all the world like an albino raisin,
seems to hover, bound only by that yellow globe above it.

"That's the last vestige of The King. Only $500.
You know, each cell has everything that you need
to make a whole person. You could clone Elvis from that wart."
A crowd gathers in awe, imagining
the million tiny possibilities risen before their eyes.

Something simple happens—devotions, beliefs,
strong through some accident of conductivity—
too much salt, too little salt, in the cell spaces of the neuroconductors,
some brief spell of ball lightning rolling through our brains—
quickening an interest in the local auto mechanic,
sending us on crusades, giving us the idea for Velcro,
telling us to kill our wives, leading us forward
in blind faith, making us hear The Word
and hope that, unlike steak, we move on to Glory,
seeing, for the first time, the glistening strings of dew
in moonlight, strung all along the spider's tender lines,
leaving us shaken in the divine smell of strawberries.

Koans of a Different Order

I make it a practice to write with my finger
on every fogged motel bathroom mirror,
squeaking out messages overlooked
by hotel staff. The oils of my skin battle
water molecules for years to come,
bringing the truth to naked strangers.

Your dog will make a gruesome discovery.

The Gideons left their bible in that drawer.
You may choose to open and read it.
The millions of skin cells dusting the mattress pad,
find their way into your body with each breath,
and I am stamped across your forehead
as you face your naked self in the mirror.

If you can hear your heart beating, there is a problem.

You lean close to line your eyes, trim your nose hair,
check the back of your tongue for mucous,
or your neck for hickies. We will always have our moments.
And so it should be. This is how the truth comes
upon you, when you are naked, staring and startled.

Saliva is a carcinogen when swallowed over time.

Time is catching you. Once it overtakes you,
there is nothing. Subtract the hours in this room
from the hours you have left. Go and get that book
from the drawer. Tear two pages out for each heartbeat.
When the two covers touch, you're gone.

Mistakes You Might Make in Spanish but Probably Wouldn't in English

Order a soap sandwich with cheese.
Confuse fingernails and nipples . . .
asking the manicurist to smooth, moisturize,
and paint your nipples "Just Right Pearl White"
(to go with your scarf, of course). Remind her to leave
them long enough to play the guitar, at least on the right.
Then announce, formally, that you are pregnant
because of these mistakes.

Request a sturdy homosexual or a duck
to raise your car because your portly, bald
tires encountered a sustained prick
and are just hissing themselves to death.

RELIC

I paid a quarter once
to lick the pickled hand of Jesus—
no, just a friend of Jesus—
no, the jar, not the actual hand.

The hand bumped heavy against the glass,
making those sounds that you hear with your chest,
and swirled in its own snowstorm of flesh.
I chose to believe. I chose to trust.

It was an easy trade, really, just a quarter and a quick
flick of the tongue for all the luck I would ever need.

THE PROPAGANDA OF MEMORY

You stand in the photo, all khaki and gleam,
where the sun found you grinning
around the stump of a cigar, holding
a wooden friar ransacked
from a French churchyard.
In the field of smoke-banked light behind you,
in the rubble of gas masks and shell casings,
helmets sparkle, and the leftovers of battle
bend to the inevitable will of forgetfulness.
The breeze lifting your hair has lost
the stale smell stolen from the mouths
of dead men, and this you,
drawn together by light, silver
particles suspended in emulsion,
is freed from the thickness of the scene, frozen
in the twitch of a photographer's finger,
leaving you remembering this moment
the same way that glass remembers sand.

THE MATH OF ICE

Before a rare hard freeze in South Georgia, my father
set out the sprinkler. It sprayed our monkey bars
all night and covered them in striated ice, like baleen.

Next morning the farm was clean. The trees
stopped making sense, shifted by the surprise of ice,
and the barn wavered through the glaze.

I climbed inside the monkey bars and sat,
surrounded by slow melting, by the sound
of water changing shape. I'm not sure

how soon the smells came back,
the prick of ammonia and rot
from the chicken houses down the road,

but when I was called inside for lunch,
the white meringue had dissolved back into mud.

THE HEART'S ARCHEOLOGY

On some fundless expedition,
you discover it beneath
a pyracantha bush
carved from the hip bone
of a long-extinct herbivore
that walked the plains on legs
a story tall. An ocarina of bone
drilled and shaped laboriously
with tools too soft to be efficient
by one primitive musician
spending night after night
squatting by the fire.
No instrument of percussion:
place this against your lips,
fill it from your lungs to sound
a note-winding double helix, solo
and thready, calling to the pack.

Fire Blight

His valley of dreaming pears, his Bartlett, his Anjou,
calls to him, calls him to harvest but his orchard still sleeps.

At the full-white bud stage, the fire blight struck
turning his trees black, flower by flower.

I trimmed and tarred the early-blooming branches
to stop the spread, took down three rows of trees on each side.

The black stumps shone among the white fallen petals.

And still his trees don't rest. They bloom again and again
and wither, each branch atrophied, a shepherd's crook.

I told him plant Moonlight, plant Maxine,
the resistant strains, like me. But no. He loves

the freckled backs, the graceful globe of the Bartlett.
He loves the constant green of the Anjou, its gloss.

LAST LETTER HOME

From my cabin I send my heart to crouch
amid the speckled grouse that pepper
the bushes beside my mother's stone.

I dream now not of wealth and island girls
but of the joy of an apple's flesh,
halved and weeping.

Last month we sailed into the still latitudes
where the heavy movements of horses
mean only meat, and water greens
in the holding tank, and the deck swells
as its grain gives over to smoothness.

Always I wake to thirst and the edge
of an unmoving horizon, my hammock
swaying over a desert of water.

ENTER THE NAGGING

It's inadvertent. Some small question during an elevator ride
sends your head on an independent safari.

"Excuse me,"

you say to the gnomish pilot guiding your cerebellum down-river,
in search of the name of the singer of "Lay Your Head on My Pillow,"
"I am taking a mid-term. Can we leave this until later?"

The boat stops, sets anchor. It swings around, swaying, a fat
pendulum. The answer is Petrarch.

Lay your warm and tender body

close to mine. Who would make that into Muzak anyway? I remember

the sunglasses he wore, and a hat. Name sounds like
a car maker . . .
rhyme scheme
of a curtal sonnet is . . . Fender. Freddy Fender!

Mine Ponies

The light which puts out our eyes is darkness to us.

—THOREAU

And so they went down, down below the fields,
the fields where the wind leaves its trail on bended
heads of golden wheat—went down

before they were broken to the bit or the trace,
before their balls dropped, their hips widened to foal,
before the velvet of their muzzles coarsened.

In the mine, darkness and dust work together
to muffle and meld all things until animals, men, machines
become a single sighing beast

that slumbers and starts, bumping along the dented walls.
When, after years of labor, the ponies surface,
they have forgotten how to graze

and cower in their stalls, lost
without that dust-dimmed world,
the sweet tightness of the shaft.

As a Boy in the Shetland Islands, I Studied Homer by Lamps Made of Burning Birds

My forefathers killed to live. But even as a boy
in the Shetlands, I thought the carnelian
gurgle of the slaughtered sheep, their tangled eyelashes,
their matted copper heat, beautiful.

And I loved to read by the ruddy glow of sputtering fat
of the campfires around Achilles,
warming the Lorica on his breastplate,
and I could see myself in that fabled company.

Later, sick of the rustic life, I wanted
my own light, my own lamps,
so I began to make them from sea birds.
I smothered them, holding their heads in my mouth
and compressing their breasts, not damaging
their thin necks so they could stand straight
like soldiers, their feet anchored in bases of clay.
Gently, gently, I held them
as I held myself through open trousers
gazing at the sea, just like Achilles.

I am far away from all that now, but I know myself
like a turtle knows its shell—
the bister above me luminous as a star.

Dark Boy

In the woods the clawed things would not stop for him.
As they loped along their path, they rolled him, scratched him,
pierced him. Not for intention. Not for malice.

They noticed him so little that they did not vary their gait
but flowed over him as if he were a log, or downed branch,
some thing added to the path as invisible to them as church steeples

are to carp. So he broke the stiff small branches from pines.
Tore handfuls of the green needles that cut the creases of his palms
if not gripped tightly enough, that wept sap, that clung to him,

stuck skin to skin and smelled of Christmas, of sauerkraut, of the hair color
his mother used. He rubbed their stickiness on his face and tore

the needles until the branches were bare. Then bound them to his own fingers
one on one on one on another on another on all the long bones
until they formed claws, ragged uneven claws, brittle claws, weak claws.

Again he waited upon the path. Again they came and flowed over him.
The boy sagged, unable to follow. He knew the direction. His body knew
the way as it knew when to breathe. Having not fur, having not claws,

he could go, could not join. And so he left his perfect world
of fur, of forgetting through motion, of belonging
and went to his mother's house where something
was burning. Something was always burning.

Smoke slipped from the oven and obscured the china faces,
hid the blue and white beauty of the leaning plates.

Mr. Turnbill to the Loggerheads

The descent to Avernus is easy, the gate of Pluto stands open night and day;
But to retrace one's steps, to return to the upper air . . .
— VIRGIL

On nights when there was no moon and the Louisiana darkness
made the tannin-stained water of Lake Bistineau
an onyx eye lashed with cypress and moss,

he stood in his tweeds—hat and coat—cuffs and calves
slicked with mud, stood redolent with the swamp
and called their low names, called until

at last they rose, parting the dark water
with heads marked by battle, by outboard motors,
their eyes unblinking examining him:

looking at his own lashless eyes, his knobbed head bulging
above the tumor, large as the stone of a cling peach.
Still as his students they watched, waiting,

and so he gave them Dido, the sadness in her eyes, her desire,
her hall of suitors. And gave them bees, how to husband the hive,
how to steer by the low star, all in the Latin he loved.

Lately he dreamed of his Grandfather,
of rattling down dirt roads, of all the dogs that chased him,
muzzles frozen in rictuses of joy. But now he stood his ground

orating, his voice booming above the black water,
and as he moved toward the end, his and Dido's, the loggerheads
were listening, their backs stepping stones across the river, bound

beyond time and language. *Hoc opus; hic labor est.*
This is the task; this is the work to be done.

Toward Lungfish

1.

My sister and I rescued eight yearlings
that were left neglected in a field, trash ponies.

Someone left a halter on one and his skin grew over it
until the halter shape seemed a part of him,

an extra ridge, another bony orbit. After we cut it out
you could still see the path, the place it made beneath the skin.

2.

From the end of the last furrow,
the farthest furrow, the one closest
to the woods, I found this flint spearhead
chipped sharp and unpredictable
as a razor. Maybe in contempt
for all the pressure it took to make it.
So damned brittle, it breaks to form the edge.

3.

Only, in a mud hut in Africa, on the bed of a long-dried lake
where lungfish sleep for years in bricks, cocooned,
is it possible to start again.
When the rain comes, and it will come, a gully-washer
big enough to make the flaked earth sigh,
the mud softens and they wake, shift, writhe,
freed to roam this newest lake, without memory,
moving through the yielding blue light.

SCARS

1.

Here is where I cut myself.
Bicep. Horizon of the nipple. The skin
puckers, lips perpetually waiting.
The white-handled knife
is long gone but the purple ridges remain,
tighten to a kiss when I fold my arms.

2.

I think of it as a fossil
from the pre-metastatic era.
The ridges humping the skin on my thigh
trouble your fingers like a knobby starfish
or the business end of a sea cucumber.
The hardness in the center is my large
leg bone. This thing went deep.

3.

Before I knew she was crazy,
before I slept with the dogs on top of the attic door,
which opened up, to be safe, for our first date,
I took her to the quarry on my Yamaha Seca
to swim and picnic. I was walking the bike down
the loose rock path to the edge of the water
when she took off her shirt and her shorts
and she beckoned. It was nothing really, but to me
it seemed like a promise, my first promise,
and watching her I slid down, fell
beneath the motorcycle.
The muffler burned me to the meat.
I couldn't cry but I couldn't stay,
and I rode all the way back to Athens
with the wind worrying the wound.

EMT CLASS

"All types of filth are represented in the human body. Don't think excrement,
think shit." My instructor popped those t's and looked right at me.
Sixty percent will flunk out before the class is over.
Another fifteen percent will fail the boards.
Most of my classmates were firemen
working for the pay upgrade: First Responder to EMT.
I was working my second programming job,
ready for a career change. We gave each other IVs,
practiced CPR on sour-smelling torsos
with gaping mouths and gray tongues,
studied the Brady guide, the way cerebrospinal fluid and blood
separate on gauze to make a bull's-eye in skull fractures.
The sixty percent and more fell away, but the tests were easy.
I was made for this. Able to ignore vomit on my glasses,
to be transfixed by penetrating trauma,
to know that eight on the pain scale makes people crap their pants,
so no matter how much they say it hurts, no shit no sympathy.

CPR

The sound of ribs is glaciers calving.
It's a sound more felt than heard.
I listen to them dive, slivering
against each other.

Inside her, the work carried out
in darkness has stopped,
and the action of cardiac muscle
is replaced by the rig of my body
pumping from the fulcrum of my hips.

What does she see through those ruined eyes—
the sixty-watt bulb above the medicine shelves,
a dwarf sun haloed and muted? Or me squatting
in her bathroom, huffing through the nausea of a hangover,
the anxiety of taking this overtime shift, coaxing her body
into pairing that last, single breath?

TRAILER FIRE

Finally, an alarm; no longer an emergency, just a removal.
The mobile home was half gone, roughed and sooted.

Stan and I went in with full gear and oxygen, a gurney and body bag.
I could smell it through the mask, a new smell, peanut butter cooking
on an overheated curling iron, the smell of fat and hair.
I took the feet, Stan the shoulders. On three. We lifted.

Expecting him to be heavy, and not wanting to be weak,
the only woman in the firehouse, I pulled hard.
But most of him had melted and fused with the sofa. He tore
and came away in parts.

The report would read "Decedent caudally separated."
Stan wrote that way in reports. When it happened,
Stan's eyes turned white all around, then he vomited into his mask.
And for an instant, I felt the lightness and confusion, then I was clear.
I led Stan outside and helped to bag the cushions, the pieces.

There had been a rightness to the moment, above everything,
the way a guitar string comes into tune:
sometimes you can hear the harmonic,
sometimes you feel it when it comes.

To Suffocate Gladly in the Air

One parasite that lives in birds of prey begins in fish.
It makes them lighter than their brethren, more visible,
and controls their brains, gives pleasure and desire:
to surface, to flaunt themselves, to rise
to that moment of claws, of puncture and suffocation.

And I believe these worms are merciful.

The water's surface breaks into diamonds,
the fish lifts toward the sun, into a joy,
wind on its scales, soaring. Soaring.

WAKING UP WITH RETROFITTED EYES

Waking, I heard a knock at the window.
I was in a windowless room and I thought there was sky.
A sky obscured by shingles of dried cod, a sea covered
with pine needles smelling of turpentine, the foam churned brown.
At the dock, Portuguese ships loading the fish. The sailors
shouldering stacks of bacalao.
                              But then a moaning,
a murmuring, the nurse's questions. The pain drove the sea away.

Where did they go, my salt cod, the fish of my dreams?
Where are my pine needles, my sailors, my surf?

Ah, in a minute, you. I know the smell of you,
beneath the alcohol, the nurse's perfume, your scent
is the trail I'll follow back home, my eyes bandaged
like a rabbit's foot.

On the other side of the curtain, a woman whose glass eye
has been refitted. They change the socket
not the eye, and the eye itself is just a shield, not round
as you would imagine, but convex. It snuggles
into the notch the surgeon carves.
It hints at roundness, it lies
                              beneath the lid, slick.
My own dry tongue clicks on the roof of my mouth,
Trying to tell someone you are here with me.

AT THE CHEMOTHERAPY CLINIC

1.

Because they put the bald kid next to me,
I know his prognosis is good. He's reading comics,
and doesn't look like you would expect.
Not Lex Lutherish. His small head
is semi-saurian with a dash of buzzard,
scaled by dry skin obscured by wisps of red.

People struck by lightning are not what you think.
I saw a picture of someone like that once.
His chest was feathered indigo, tattooed
with tracings of vein and downy capillary.

Animals that survive being struck by lightning
aren't eaten by the others. They wander around
free from predation. The catch is, they don't know it.
They still dart and slink and start in the night.

2.

There is a curtain, yes. At the top is an inch
of machine-made lace with square holes.
There are eight holes down and sixteen holes across
between each loop. The curtain does not reach the floor. It floats
just above it. It floats just over the top of the shoe.
I know them by their shoes. There is a small stain of Betadine
near the top of the curtain. It is shaped like New Guinea.

I love the pink roll of your ear.

Malignancy is the story of cells gone wrong. A revolt.
A revolution. Cells begin to replicate. They make you sick.

The chairs are turquoise or mint green or orange
or some color that survives the seventies. They sweat us.
They sweat me. My skin sticks to them and they hold.

I love your cool mouth.

In the chairs, I drink then vomit. Water dripping,
water in bags, water in glass, water on stone,
water soaking into the ground.

I love the moons of your fingernails.

I go home. I vomit. I chew Tums. I eat saltines straight from their sleeve
and stare down the soup in the cupboard. I kiss your cool mouth.

THE MOVING DARK

I know what God did with the darkness.
He took it and chained it inside us.
It is the red sadness.
It moves and it seeks the light.

It presses and promises and threatens.
It leaks from our eyes and our noses and mouths.

It whispers wet-hot like meat on our breath.

STUD-HORSE DIAMONDS AND THE MOON

The stallion's wound was large enough
to hold a cantaloupe or newborn child.
A hunk of flesh hung down and when I bound it
back in place,
it didn't quite belong, but settled,
humped and hollowed, as if I'd tried
to plug the moon back into the Pacific, fitting
crater to coral reef, stretching the Mare Imbrium
over the Mariana Islands and stitching it in place.

Time hardened the black volcanic sand and lunar dust
into a scar. Now the roan slants toward his hollowed shoulder,
orbits his paddock and the rusted Chevy whose windshield
his leg plunged through. In the moat of scab
between the puckered edge and peninsula
of plugged flesh, rising points appear:

the wound weeps diamonds of green glass
into the stall, along the hayrack, and onto the grass
when his nose is plunged into the water trough.

CONSTANCY

She tends her oven in the quiet forest. She sugars
her candied sills until they glisten.
She tends the fire, and she waits.
She promises herself not to eat the children.
But she can't balance loneliness against desire.
Each roasted digit, each poached knuckle,
each stewed thigh will be a thing of braised delight.
She bends and tends and cleans the stoop.
She lights the windows.

Sheet Metal Metronome

When does the goal become a curse?
We had a dog once, Bella. She stared. She sat on the porch
my father made of sheet metal laid over a brick foundation,
stared at the moon and gonged her tail in a constant rhythm.
It was worse in the summer when the windows were open.
In my narrow bed, I set up equations
to calculate those thumps,
                        the miles
                                traveled in wags,

but
        the numbers, no matter how high, never seemed enough.

FORCING IT

1.

The summer I was eight, we raised biddies,
five hundred yellow fluff-balls on stiff toothpick legs,
huddled at the feeder or in the corner.
The first night in the brooder, one lost a toe,
another was opened up on its back to the bones.

I checked every edge, every wire-end for a cruel point,
and I painted them with Gentian Violet,
any with a dark spot, or starting feathers,
but each morning more were stripped—
their gizzards glistening gray and pink—

and still running around, too stupid
to know they were dead. But I understood.
At night I cut and measured
horse bandages to flatten
my breasts when I slept.

2.

He marks the killings on the kitchen calendar,
red circle just after the last corn is cut
and the hogs, the final beans, frost
tracings on the collard leaves. Meanwhile
the chickens can scratch away in the yard,
and I know when it's coming, the smell of scald,
the scaled lids half closed, the combs lightening to pink.
No need, before that day, to dodge and flinch
the way I do, not knowing when his anger
will drive his hand, no need to push and push until I get it:
my lip, my teeth, his hand, my blood, my terms.

THE NAMING OF THE BODY

I was a good child. I waited
and I listened, and I learned
about the nature of things.
The way the male box turtle's plastrum
is cupped, the fork in the shell above
its thicker tail. Modifications so he could fit,
so he could mate without rocking away.

I thought that there would be a change.
At some point I would
change and grow
to be a man, to take my place with a wife.
When I asked my mother at five what my name would be,
when I would be changed, she cried. And now
I know
        I will die in this body.

FOR THE BOY I NEVER WAS

The men lit the fires in the corners of the field. When Rob was old enough,
they gave him a can and a torch and set him to burning. It starts like this,

the division. Labor. Knowledge. Scars and calluses. The post
between Grandfather and Father, beers, and fire. Soot-gilded faces

alchemic in red light. But Rob dangled his legs from the tailgate,
holding an Old Milwaukee he would not drink—

Nor when it was done would he walk the field
passing the animals as black as the ground,

twisted among the burnt stubble as in the stories
he heard them tell, stories of war:

Animals thin enough won't burn.
Flames starve on their bodies.

Rob makes his family and life with other men:
they have the licenses to all the secrets.

Now, only the women are left to burn the fields.
And we don't know why the coyotes have come back.

Our dogs take up with them and hunt, mate, probably die.
The old yellow bitch stares at the woods, listening

to the pack, the barks, the howls.
She trembles and strains, pacing the edge

of the cleared land. But she won't go to them:
we are the ones who feed her.

Spring Diving

Michael's little brother hung himself with a belt
from their bunk bed. Because he was too tall,

he folded his legs and hooked the toes of his sneakers
on the footboard of the lower bunk. With his arms and head down,

he looked as if he was jumping into a spring, the spring
at the back of their land, the one with the small opening,

the one that is very, very deep.
He killed himself in third grade.

Michael's family raised tomatoes in North Carolina.
They lived in a log house their daddy built from a kit.

They only had money once a year,
the rest of the time they made do with credit.

So the tennis shoes that Michael saved,
the ones his little brother was wearing,

were Converse knock-off, not real Chuck Taylors.
He helped his brother lace them

so that the laces weren't crossed but were parallel, like ribs.
He called it performance lacing.

Michael didn't tell me he was gay for over a year
even though he knew I was. He told me so he could show me the shoes.

We took the same class at Kennesaw State—
built dulcimers out of cardboard, learned some fiddle tunes.

He could only strum one way, so I tuned mine differently:
same positions, a little harmony.

SLINGSHOT

V for victory, virtue, Venus,
the legs of Venus. And this pebble
in the leather purse is pinched
between my fingers. I pull it slowly,
deliberately, to increase the tension.
Breathe in and hold. Ignore the trembling.
Steady. Wait. Wait.
Then let go.

GORGON

With bait-bucket shiners I'd saved to feed your hair,
I drew you to my own small pond
pebbled with frogs and fish that dared
to look above the water, Medusa
of Loneliness. I have no wish to look—

I hate you, I hate you for fucking
Poseidon in the temple.
And I also hate this loathsome heat we make,
the rattling breaths, my chest turned wicked and weak
as a bird's nest from a hardwood forest.

Remembering Melville's Obituary at Four in the Morning

My love is as pale as tofu. I can see her back
in almost total darkness. Her skin catches the barest hint of light,

the only white on the field—watching it
is like looking into the sea at night.
I can't remember what actually happens in the end
of *Moby Dick*. I do know what happened to Melville.

He died, at home, his obituary almost unnecessary.
Most people thought him long dead.

FRUIT AND WAR

What strange photographs: you in every one. Eating
pomegranates, gooseberries, peaches, one strand of hair
across your cheek, tip in the corner of your mouth
a stretched strand of caramel.

My room is littered with posed pictures: the proof of life.
Me with this teacher, that acquaintance, someone else's children,
me with you, and me between two cardboard llamas.

The stairway between us is an unbalanced scale,
the breakfast table a no-man's land, the rutted mud
of Verdun—sucking, separating, the trenches uncrossable.

TAKING TEA IN THE SWEET POTATO GARDEN

We watch bees weave among the tangled vines,
legs heavy with balled pollen,

a stream of them flowing between the rows
as we mix honey into our tea. Homer, you say,

wrote of honey bees flying through storms,
carrying stones for ballast. How can a bee

know its stone mate? Imagine the bee
picking up that stone with legs

like hard candy, scrabbling for purchase.
Imagine the deepening murmur of wings

pulling against weight, ten thousand leaves shivering
as the storm comes. Keep the dog,

you have a fence. But without its stone, the bee
climbs, dives, unable to hold altitude, unable

to remember its own steady weight.
I will be drinking tea alone among these yams,

my own legs strangely heavy without the stone.

OFFERINGS

Today I made a list of everything I would cut off
if you would stay. Tiny offerings of flesh,
gibbets of gristle: earlobe, nipple, pinky, hand.
I could cut them off with the pruners if I took them all
from the right side. I would whittle myself away
for just a bit more of you, for just a promise,
the shadow of a promise.

BOURBON VESPERS

My tongue bleeds while the wrens trill to dusk in the backyard.
The blood tastes of pennies, of rust. The bourbon stings when I hold it in my mouth.

I spit it back into the glass and it is black, a squid's trail. Night has taken the birds
to roost and quiet when I finish the drink, black and all, and take more from the bottle.

The world is gone or as good as gone.

Fourteen Days

1. Knot

When I raise my right arm, tension—
something connected where it should not be—
gum between sole and sidewalk
It does not ease with stretches.
When I probe with my fingers and find the node,
it sounds an internal bass note. I hear it
and the house hums in the background
and the neighbor is blowing leaves in the yard
and the clink of the poorly loaded dishwasher
stutters before finding its cadence once more.

2. Wish

And so the little wooden dog came to life. It chased sticks through the verge,
quick and smooth on its wooden wheels. But when the boy pulled it home

with the knotted cotton string, the little wooden dog would not eat.
It would not drink. It only rolled around and around

the braided oval kitchen rug with two wheels on the rug
and two wheels on the tile. Soon the wheels began to squeak

and the wood turned rough and gray and the little wooden dog trembled
as if rolling through the tumult of a great storm. So the boy returned

to his knot of wishes and rubbed the smooth head until it was warm.
He wanted to fix this, to clarify his wish to bring contentment

to the little wooden dog so it could roll once more on the verge.
But still the little wooden dog worried the braided rug.

Then it tipped over, rattled once, and was still.

3. *Depth*

What can you tell about a bruise just looking at it,
at the darkening blood stopped in its rotation?
For depth or severity, you need to know
when it happened, how it happened,
how long the color deepened,
how long blood spread beneath the skin,
how long the tissue absorbed the blow.

4. The Day Possum Died

The day Possum died, we did nothing.
We did nothing because Possum had died this way before.
Twice before. This is where the waiting comes in.

Old Pos could snap into a coma over anything.
Once it was the theme song from *The Good, The Bad, and The Ugly*.
Its crescendo did Possum in. I imagine it was the whistling,
the mother of all hawks descending upon him. Once
it was my father, clapping his hands sharply over a Gator fumble.
He actually died in the Browning box that served as his bedroom.
My mother made us wait three days to bury him.

5. The Things I Can Do

At 44 and fat I can walk into a field and clear it, alone.

If I dropped halfway from heat stroke, I would wake
and continue until it was finished. I have a talent
for ignoring pain; bleeding blisters, torn muscles,
broken bones in my foot. I can push through the hedgerows.

But these things are different. How did these matters of the body
move inside to wake my chest, to make them part of imagination? And
what
of it, what of the moth-dusting of wings, the things
the mind tends for the heart. How have they been enlivened?

If you took a bat to me, or hammer, I would not cry
for the bruises or the stitches. What hurts is your will,
your will to swing away.

6. Cutting the Hay

As I move down the field the hawks ride my right shoulder,
then dive and feed when the tractor flushes
the rabbits from their warrens, the rats from their runs.
The thundering, the tremble, the roar
freezes some: those the blades mist into the drying piles.
They had a choice. They could have run through the uncut field
to the woods. They did not need to dart into the open;
into the eyes of the hawks. The ones that brave
the clearing, that choose sun over shade, are taken, quickly.

7. Imagination

After my grandmother died I broke a little.
I broke the swivel that shifts your eyes from inside to out.
I know because I was stuck looking inside.

I saw the people punch the time clock at Kimbrell-Stern.
The people who drain and wash the dead, not the nice ones,
the ones who do hair and makeup. The ones I saw wore plastic aprons

and went home to their wives smelling of chemicals and rot.
They drink coffee and laugh. They left my grandmother on the table
five minutes longer than she needed to be. They left the sheet off of her.

They were rough and shoved the big hollow needle hard into her thigh
into the artery there. They turned on the pump. And I could not look away.
I could not turn outside, not even at the wake, not even for my mother's tears.

8. On Just Holding Steady

Just think of this moment of this one
breath, of its declension. Try snapping
a rubber band on your wrist repeatedly.
Try to raise a welt, a bruise, a blood blister. Try counting
to ten, then back down to zero, an octave
plus two, a child's slide whistle, the sound
of a carton fall. Pull out your eyebrows, eyelashes,
pubic hair, whatever is long enough for you to grasp.
Then try to think again without imagining the venom
of the box jellyfish, the only toxin
that stops your heart—clenched.

9. *Flaws of the Giant Clam*

The clam is large enough to hold me like a lover.

It is bright blue inside. The color of its shell, sand.

Looking down at it is like looking through a torn curtain

into the sky. The shell stays open unless light is blocked.

A fish can eat it alive as long as no shadows are cast on its heart.

10. Closet Monster

The closet monster came first to the hospital.
I fell asleep during *The Inn of the Sixth Happiness.*
When I woke, someone had turned off the lights
and it was easing its way out into the room.
It was walnut-headed and clicking and swimming
free in the shadows. The clicks I can only imagine
are chitenous jaws slick as hard candy. It's always hungry.
It's impatient. It keens and rocks when others approach.
It should disappear when the lights are turned on, but it doesn't.
It becomes a wastrel thing of strings and sticks,
a secret, a fixture.

11. *How We Know Things*

Digestion remained a mystery
until a duck-hunting accident in 1652.
Alexis, Canadian, was blasted in the stomach by a shotgun,
leaving part of a lung and most of his digestive tract exposed.
It took a year for the wound to heal into a fistula—
It closed, but not entirely, like a well-used ice-fishing hole.

At Fort Ticonderoga, Dr. Beaumont dipped in food on a string
and documented the effects of the stomach. Zealously he recorded
his findings, even making note of the effects of temperature.
Not much was said of Alexis.

12. *The Light the Eyes Make*

On my father's sailboat in the San Blas Archipelago,
caught beneath the black bowl of a clouded sky,
I sleep on a hammock suspended between forestay
and mast. If I think slow enough, or large enough,
I can track the *Kestyll's* movement on the anchor, the swaying
that will put her bow to the wind. If I try to see, try to resolve
any object in the darkness, my eyes hurt as if I have been reading
for hours. My mind is all alone in the dark.

This is where the werewolf comes from, trickster gods, tumors,
betrayals, all the rot-breathed leviathans I can raise.
I can see my monster crouched above me,
sea wind blowing its slaver into silver loops.
But I can't see the deck, or the cleat with its troubled figure eight.

Then coming toward me in the sea a dotted line of light,
light like a burning yak-butter candle, the skittery light of animal fat
on fire in a cave. Over instant coffee in broken Spanish I ask the mate.

It's either a squid or the light your eyes make.

13. Believing

For seven years I have walked this park,
and I have looked for the beavers.
My mother walked here twice and saw them.
I think of them, lodge close to the city,
four blocks from the Waffle House,
surrounded by subdivisions, beavers under siege.
The park maintenance people put ten-gauge wire
around the trunks of the dogwoods.

At Easter, I walked my friend through.
Showed her the lodge, the hatched stick roof,
the one tree worked on by a woodpecker,
the place where the geese nest. "They're gone,"
she said. And so I looked, I touched the trees
where they had been, the symmetrical
grooves, the flayed wood waists: gray.
All gray. But I still look for them.

14. *Prayer*

Make me stone. Fill my lungs
with earth, my stomach with water.
Make me the pit of the fruit that breaks
teeth. God, grant me not peace. Let me be
a vessel of rage, claw and fang.

ACKNOWLEDGMENTS

Grateful acknowledgment is made to the editors of the following journals and anthologies, in which these poems appeared:

asspants: "Biology Lesson," "Used Saves"
CAIRN: "Hardware Disease"
The Cortland Review: "Fourteen Days"
Grand Street: "Mine Ponies"
Inch: "Slingshot"
Kenyon Review: "Propaganda of Memory"
New Orleans Review: "Talismans"
Poetry: "Heart's Archaeology," "Propaganda of Memory"

"Talismans" and "Mr Turnbill to the Loggerheads" appeared in *The Made Thing*, edited by Leon Stokesbury. "Talismans" also appeared in *All Shook Up*, edited by Will Clemens. "The Propaganda of Memory" and "The Heart's Archaeology" appeared in *The Southern Poetry Anthology*, edited by Paul Ruffin and William Wright.

ABOUT THE AUTHOR

MAUDELLE DRISKELL holds an M.F.A. in poetry from Warren Wilson College. Her work has been published in many literary reviews and anthologies. She is the recipient of the Ruth Lilly Fellowship, awarded by *Poetry* and the Modern Language Association.

Raised in south Georgia, Driskell lived most of her adult life in Atlanta. She now lives in Bethlehem, New Hampshire, where she is the executive director of The Frost Place, an arts organization headquartered in Robert Frost's historic home. Driskell is constantly inspired by the legacy of Robert Frost and the beauty of the landscape.

THE HOBBLEBUSH GRANITE STATE
POETRY SERIES

*HOBBLEBUSH BOOKS publishes several New Hampshire
poets each year, poets whose work has already received
recognition but deserves to be more widely known. The
editors are Sidney Hall Jr. and Rodger Martin.
For more information, visit the Hobblebush
website: www.hobblebush.com.*